# Before the Civil War

*1830–1860*

D1515947

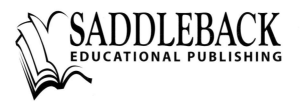

SADDLEBACK
EDUCATIONAL PUBLISHING

# Saddleback's *Graphic American History*

ISBN-13: 978-1-59905-361-5
ISBN-10: 1-59905-361-6
eBook: 978-1-60291-689-0

Printed in Guangzhou, China
0511/05-26-11

15 14 13 12 11   3 4 5 6 7 8 9

While American settlers in Oregon celebrated the treaty making that territory American, the rest of the United States was concerned with a large tract of land far to the south.

Tom Tyler was a boy who lived in Tennessee.

Say, Dad, what does G.T.T. mean?

Stands for "Gone to Texas." You fixin' to go?

Course not. But when I went to the Byes' cabin, everybody was gone and they'd written G.T.T. on the door! Why?

Well, Texas is a big tract of land next to the United States that belongs to Mexico. A lot of land, not many people.

Some people take off for Texas when they get in trouble with the law. Others, like the Byes, think they can get good land there cheap, and make more money.

Would you like to go?

I reckon I wouldn't like the rules. You have to become a Mexican citizen and join the Catholic church.

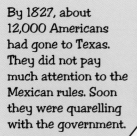

By 1827, about 12,000 Americans had gone to Texas. They did not pay much attention to the Mexican rules. Soon they were quarelling with the government.

You heard the latest from the Mexican government?

You mean the high taxes?

This is a lot worse than taxes! They've passed a law against slavery!

That's crazy! How's anybody gonna raise cotton without slaves?

They're just trying to keep us Americans out!

Stephen Austin had brought the first group of American settlers to Texas. Now the Americans talked of revolt. Austin conferred with Sam Houston, a newcomer from Tennessee.

According to Santa Anna's* latest decrees, we can't gather in groups of more than 10 people. We can't criticize the government. We can't worship as Protestants! Americans won't stand for it!

I am going to Mexico City, Sam. Surely I can work out a compromise that will satisfy both sides.

* Ruler of Mexico

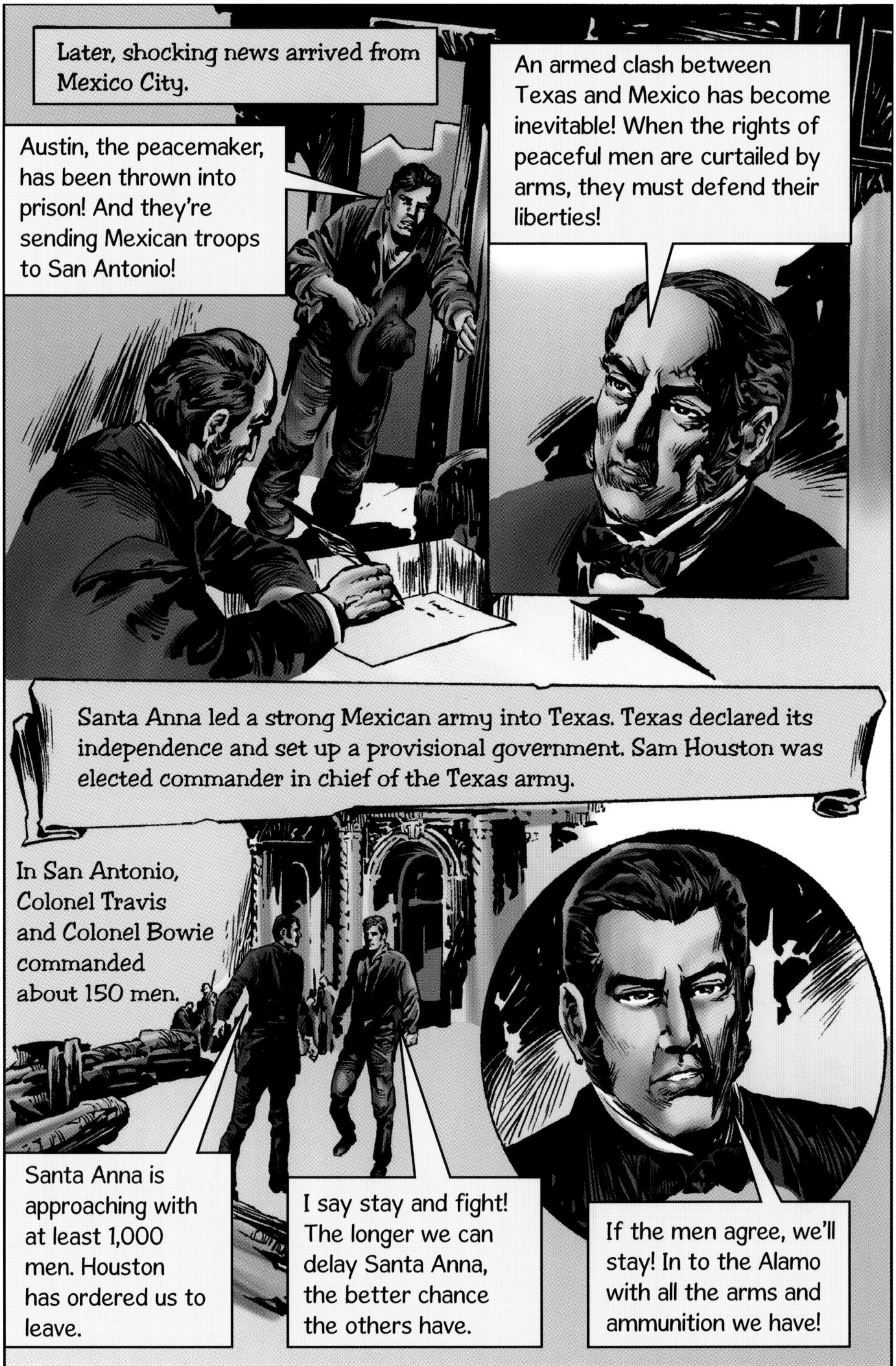
Later, shocking news arrived from Mexico City.
Austin, the peacemaker, has been thrown into prison! And they're sending Mexican troops to San Antonio!
An armed clash between Texas and Mexico has become inevitable! When the rights of peaceful men are curtailed by arms, they must defend their liberties!
Santa Anna led a strong Mexican army into Texas. Texas declared its independence and set up a provisional government. Sam Houston was elected commander in chief of the Texas army.
In San Antonio, Colonel Travis and Colonel Bowie commanded about 150 men.
Santa Anna is approaching with at least 1,000 men. Houston has ordered us to leave.
I say stay and fight! The longer we can delay Santa Anna, the better chance the others have.
If the men agree, we'll stay! In to the Alamo with all the arms and ammunition we have!

4

The Alamo was not a fort but an old Spanish mission, partly in ruins. Inside were 187 Texans—besieged by several thousand Mexicans with 12 and 18 pound cannons.

On March 6, 1836, the Alamo fell. Every man inside was killed. But they were not to be forgotten.

Houston, with only a small, poorly equipped army, worked out a strategy.

We must keep backing away until Santa Anna makes a mistake. Then we attack!

His chance came on April 21, at the San Jacinto River.

With Buffalo Bayou in front of him, and the river on his flank, Santa Anna can't maneuver. This is the trap I've wanted!

Ordering the attack, Houston led his men with a new battle cry.

Remember the Alamo, men! Remember the Alamo!

Although outnumbered two to one, the Texans routed the Mexicans, killed several hundred, captured 730 including Santa Anna. Six Americans were killed and 25 wounded.

As a prisoner, Santa Anna promised to recognize the independence of Texas. It became the Lone Star Republic. On October 22, 1836, Sam Houston became its first president. France, England, and the United States recognized the new republic. Texas applied for admission to the United States.

Then word came from Washington.

The Senate has voted down the treaty to annex Texas! The anti-slavery people are afraid of adding another slave state to the Union.

Can Texas go it alone?

Santa Anna threatens to bring his army back and reconquer us. We have no army or navy. But there is always England.

It was December 1845 before Texas legally became a state in the Union. Then Sam Houston was sent to Washington as a senator.

A note from my old friend Jamie Polk, inviting me to dinner.

The United States would not like us to become too closely tied to Great Britain!

The new president of the United States, James K. Polk, was a Tennessean. Houston went to the White House.

What's our situation with Mexico, Sam?

Santa Anna has never recognized Texas as an independent state. By annexing us, you've insulted him. He'll go to war!

I will send General Taylor and the army of the southwest to defend Texas.

Good!

Zachary Taylor, known as "Old-Rough-and-Ready," landed at Corpus Christi, Texas, with 4,000 men.

We'll proceed to the Rio Grande, 150 miles away.

Texas claimed the Rio Grande River as its border. Mexico claimed the land to the Nueces River, farther north.

Send out a scouting party of dragoons.*

In the territory between the two rivers, the dragoons were surrounded by Mexican troops.

Eleven Americans were killed, the rest wounded or captured.

* Soldiers with short muskets

General Taylor dictated a letter to the president.

In a military action, American blood was spilled on American soil!

As a result, the United States declared war against Mexico on May 13, 1846.

Taylor moved his forces 400 miles up the Rio Grande, to Camargo.

From Camargo they marched inland to Monterrey, defended by 7,000 Mexican troops under General Ampudia. For three days in the rain, the Americans fought their way house by house, street by street, in a dogged battle.

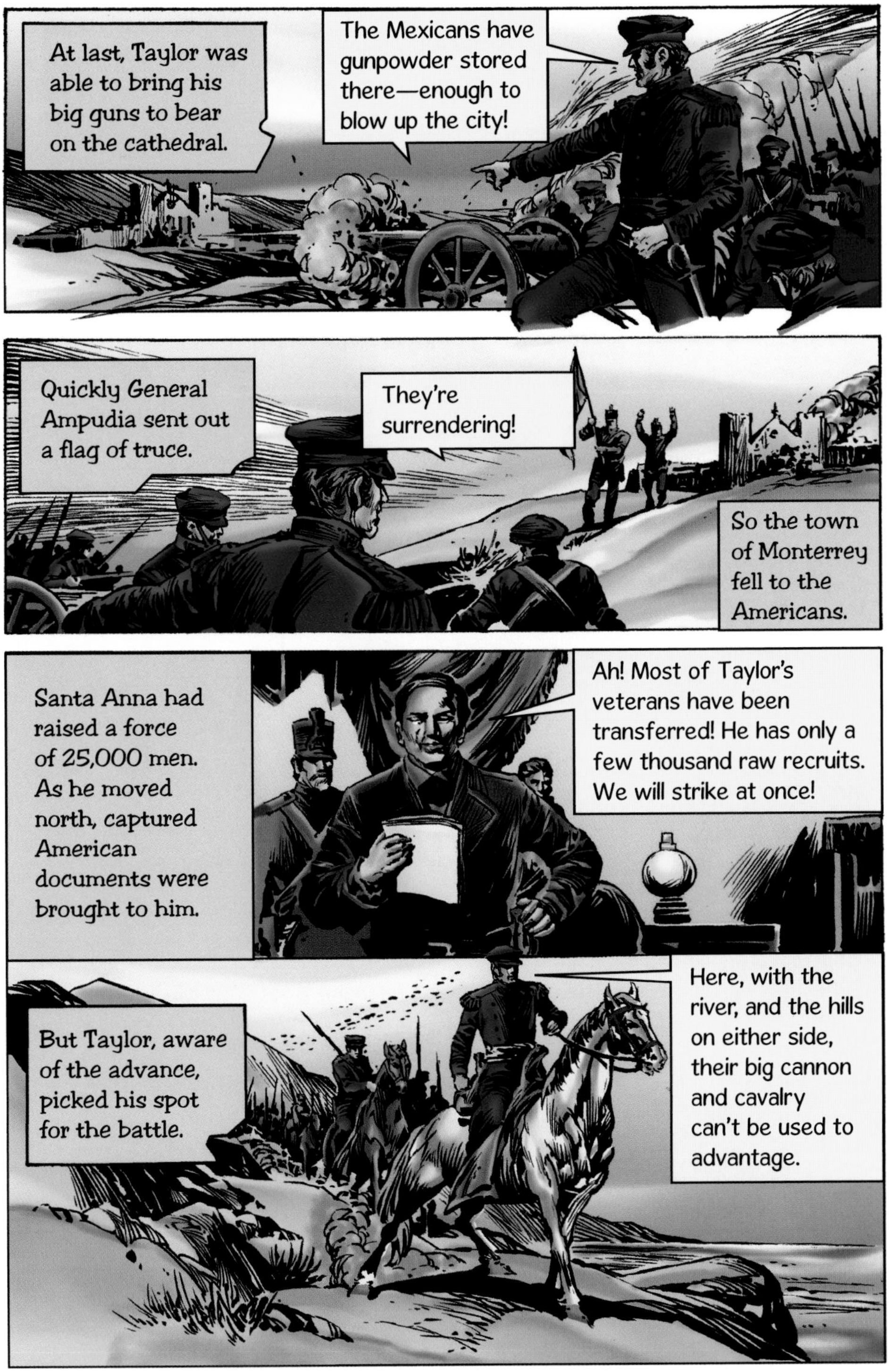
At last, Taylor was able to bring his big guns to bear on the cathedral.
The Mexicans have gunpowder stored there—enough to blow up the city!
Quickly General Ampudia sent out a flag of truce.
They're surrendering!
So the town of Monterrey fell to the Americans.
Santa Anna had raised a force of 25,000 men. As he moved north, captured American documents were brought to him.
Ah! Most of Taylor's veterans have been transferred! He has only a few thousand raw recruits. We will strike at once!
But Taylor, aware of the advance, picked his spot for the battle.
Here, with the river, and the hills on either side, their big cannon and cavalry can't be used to advantage.

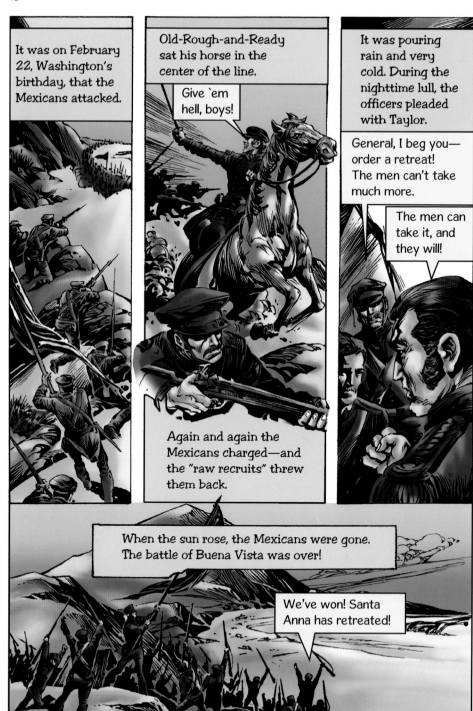

It was on February 22, Washington's birthday, that the Mexicans attacked.

Old-Rough-and-Ready sat his horse in the center of the line.

Give 'em hell, boys!

Again and again the Mexicans charged—and the "raw recruits" threw them back.

It was pouring rain and very cold. During the nighttime lull, the officers pleaded with Taylor.

General, I beg you— order a retreat! The men can't take much more.

The men can take it, and they will!

When the sun rose, the Mexicans were gone. The battle of Buena Vista was over!

We've won! Santa Anna has retreated!

Meanwhile in Washington, President Polk consulted Houston about overall strategy.

We'll only win this war by capturing Mexico City. And we'll never do that by sending a land army through the deserts and mountains.

What do you suggest, Sam?

Use the navy—a combined operation. If Veracruz could be captured, the army could strike inland from there.

We'll do it!

General Winfield Scott, known as "Old-Fuss-and-Feathers," was commander in chief. Naval vessels transported him and his force of 13,600 men to Veracruz, the strongest fortified city in the Western Hemisphere. They landed south of the city without opposition.

If they refuse to surrender, I will bombard the city from sea and from land.

Scott's guns opened up. The city guns answered.

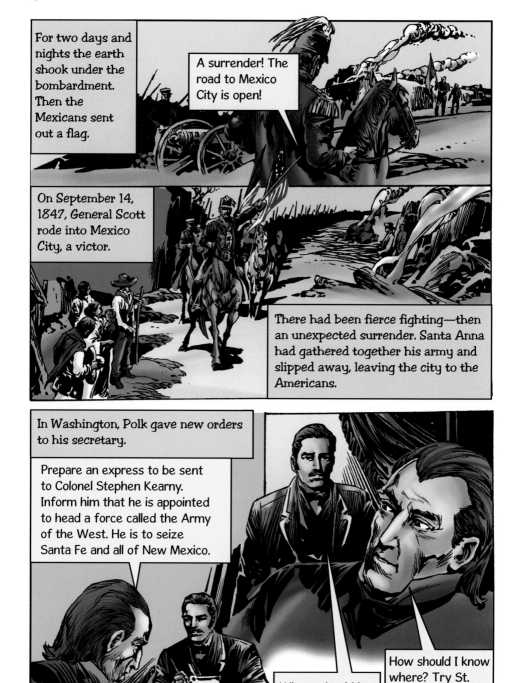

For two days and nights the earth shook under the bombardment. Then the Mexicans sent out a flag.

A surrender! The road to Mexico City is open!

On September 14, 1847, General Scott rode into Mexico City, a victor.

There had been fierce fighting—then an unexpected surrender. Santa Anna had gathered together his army and slipped away, leaving the city to the Americans.

In Washington, Polk gave new orders to his secretary.

Prepare an express to be sent to Colonel Stephen Kearny. Inform him that he is appointed to head a force called the Army of the West. He is to seize Santa Fe and all of New Mexico.

Where should it be sent? Where is Colonel Kearny?

How should I know where? Try St. Louis. Try Fort Leavenworth! But hurry.

It was at the frontier post of Fort Leavenworth that the orders reached Kearny. He talked to his quartermaster.

Major Swords, get to St. Louis for supplies—rifles, carbines, ammunition, uniforms, shoes, food...

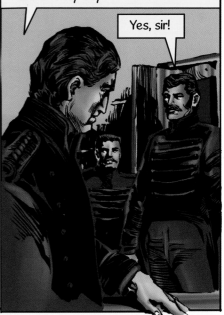

Captain Sumner, Captain Cooke—We have 1,000 volunteers arriving. You have twenty days to train them!

Yes, sir!

Just a month later, on June 30, 1846, Kearny led 1,658 troops out of Fort Leavenworth onto the long trail leading west to Santa Fe.

14

Meanwhile, on June 27, 1844, a mob gathered outside the jail at Carthage, Illinois.

We want Joseph Smith! Bring him out!

Dan Jones hurried to the governer of Illinois.

Sir, Joseph Smith and his brother are in great danger!

You are unnecessarily alarmed for the safety of your friends. The people are not that cruel.

The Smiths are American citizens! They surrendered to you when you pledged their safety. I demand your protection!

Jones returned to the jail.

No visitors for the Smiths. You'd best leave—for your own safety!

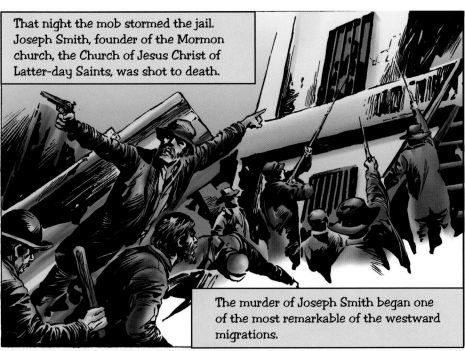

That night the mob stormed the jail. Joseph Smith, founder of the Mormon church, the Church of Jesus Christ of Latter-day Saints, was shot to death.

The murder of Joseph Smith began one of the most remarkable of the westward migrations.

Brigham Young succeeded Smith as leader of the 20,000 Mormons in Nauvoo, Illinois.

We must go west to the Rockies where there will be no neighbors and where no one else wants to live.

We have been driven ... from Ohio, from Missouri, and from Illinois because our ... neighbors would not let us live in peace.

The first Mormons left Nauvoo on February 4, 1846, crossing the ice-choked Mississippi.

Mommy, I'm scared!

I'm n-not s-scared!

Hush! God and Brother Young will look after us.

Brigham Young did his best, from helping unstick heavy wagons ...

All together—heave!

... to showing inexperienced women how to cook over a campfire.

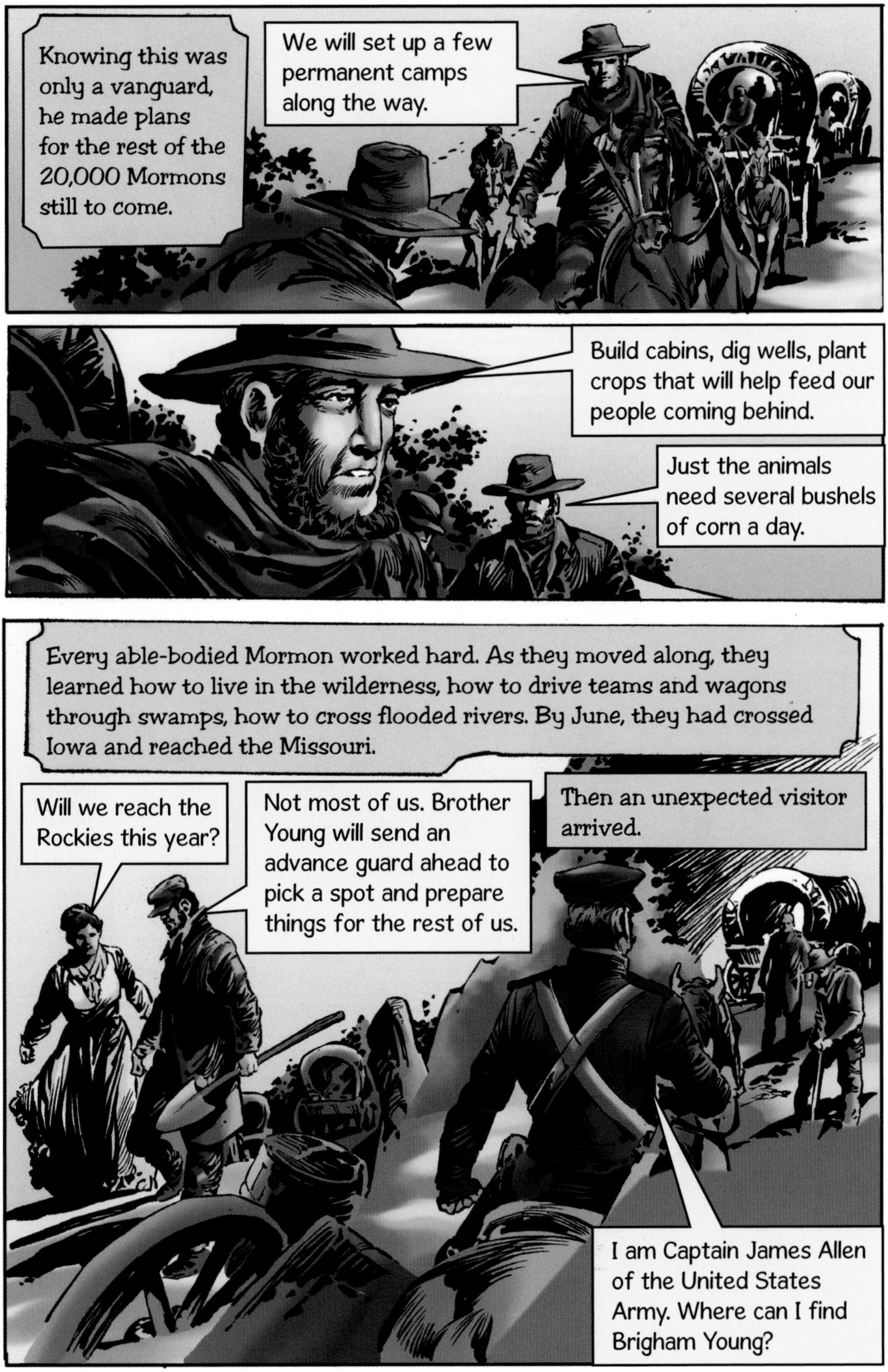
Knowing this was only a vanguard, he made plans for the rest of the 20,000 Mormons still to come.
We will set up a few permanent camps along the way.
Build cabins, dig wells, plant crops that will help feed our people coming behind.
Just the animals need several bushels of corn a day.
Every able-bodied Mormon worked hard. As they moved along, they learned how to live in the wilderness, how to drive teams and wagons through swamps, how to cross flooded rivers. By June, they had crossed Iowa and reached the Missouri.
Will we reach the Rockies this year?
Not most of us. Brother Young will send an advance guard ahead to pick a spot and prepare things for the rest of us.
Then an unexpected visitor arrived.
I am Captain James Allen of the United States Army. Where can I find Brigham Young?

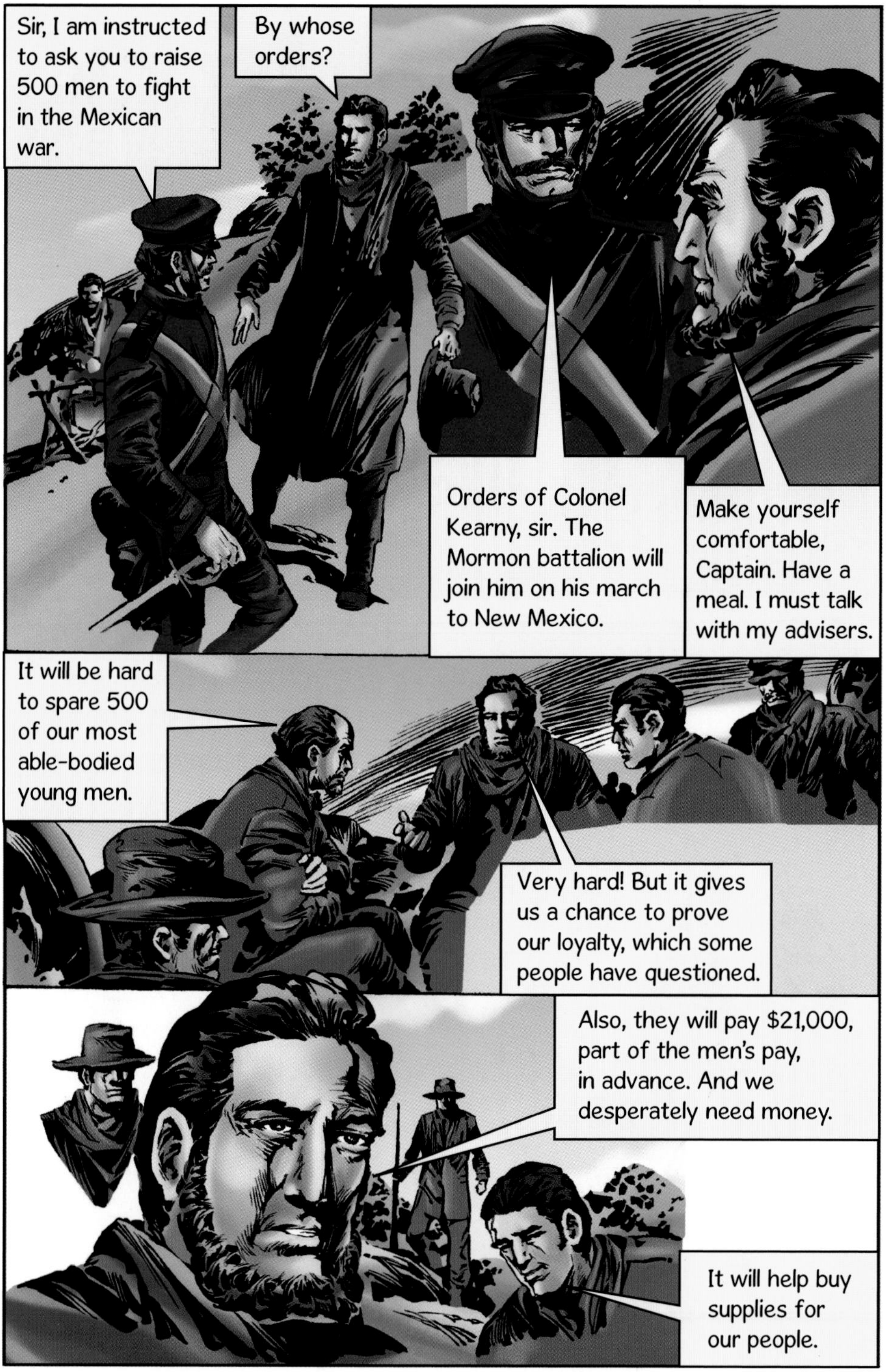
Sir, I am instructed to ask you to raise 500 men to fight in the Mexican war.
By whose orders?
Orders of Colonel Kearny, sir. The Mormon battalion will join him on his march to New Mexico.
Make yourself comfortable, Captain. Have a meal. I must talk with my advisers.
It will be hard to spare 500 of our most able-bodied young men.
Very hard! But it gives us a chance to prove our loyalty, which some people have questioned.
Also, they will pay $21,000, part of the men's pay, in advance. And we desperately need money.
It will help buy supplies for our people.

The Mormon Battalion was recruited and marched away to war. Those left behind wintered on the Missouri. In April, a carefully chosen Pioneer Company led by Brigham Young took the trail, in search of the spot in the Rockies where they could build their new civilization.

On June 27, the party crossed the Continental Divide.

The watershed of the country! All the streams to our east make their way to the Atlantic—to our west, to the Pacific!

The next day they had a visitor—Jim Bridger, most famous of the Mountain Men.

Welcome, sir! Sup with us and tell me what you know about the Salt Lake Valley.

Why, I discovered the Great Salt Lake. Been there 50 times, I reckon.

It's dry, barren, no place for a settlement! I'll give a $1,000 for the first bushel of corn grown there!

Someday I may collect that money!

We want a place no one will want to take away from us. Sounds like the Salt Lake Valley is it.

To reach it you follow the same trail the Donner party took. Just last winter, that was.

They were pushing through to California. The deep snow caught them in the mountains.

Did they make it?

No sir! Seventy-nine started. Thirty-four died—starved or froze. The survivors—well, they ate their dead friends.

Poor souls, poor souls!

The party followed Bridger's directions. In July, on the Donner party's trail, they reached a pass in the Wasatch Mountains.

Yes! This is the place!

Soon afterward they reached the valley.

Get out the plows! It may be too late for a crop this year, but we must try for one.

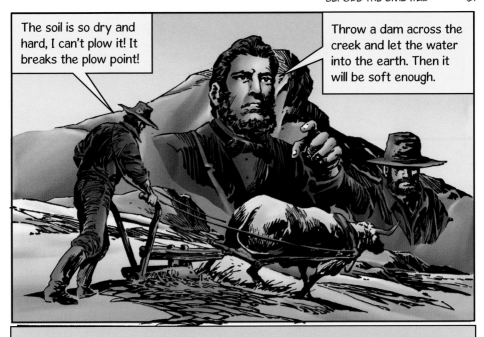

The idea worked. Later that afternoon, they were able to plow the land and plant the first crops. That rough dam was the beginning of an irrigation system that would eventually turn the whole arid valley into a fertile garden.

Like a black tide they poured down from the mountains and settled over the growing plants.

Get wet blankets, barrel staves, anything!

It's no use. The more we kill, the more there are!

Brigham Young was away and John Smith was in charge. He knew what must be done.

Only God can help us. Pray, my fellow saints. Ask His help!

In the fields, the Mormons dropped to their knees and prayed. Suddenly overhead they heard a sharp cry.

Seagulls from the Great Salt Lake!

The seagulls settled over the fields.

Are they going to eat what's left of our crops?

No—they're eating the crickets!

The gulls came by the thousands, until all the crickets were destroyed and the crops saved.

We have been saved by a miracle. We will always remember it.

Ever since, the seagull has been a revered bird to the Mormons. Today a seagull statue stands in Salt Lake City, Utah.

Gradually, through hard work and resourcefulness, the Mormons built a prosperous community. Their settlements in the West grew to 150,000 people. Salt Lake City remained the Mormon capital, and in 1896, the state of Utah was admitted to the Union.

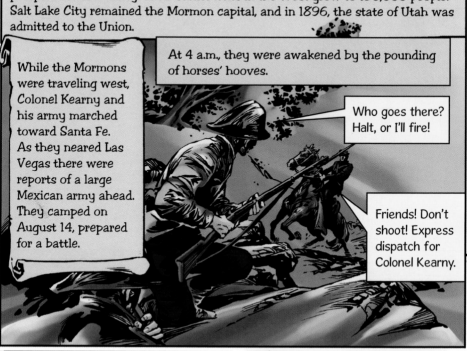

While the Mormons were traveling west, Colonel Kearny and his army marched toward Santa Fe. As they neared Las Vegas there were reports of a large Mexican army ahead. They camped on August 14, prepared for a battle.

At 4 a.m., they were awakened by the pounding of horses' hooves.

Who goes there? Halt, or I'll fire!

Friends! Don't shoot! Express dispatch for Colonel Kearny.

Bad news, sir?

No ... just more responsibility. I've been made a brigadier general.

Congratulations, sir!

Also, after taking New Mexico, we are to move on west to seize California!

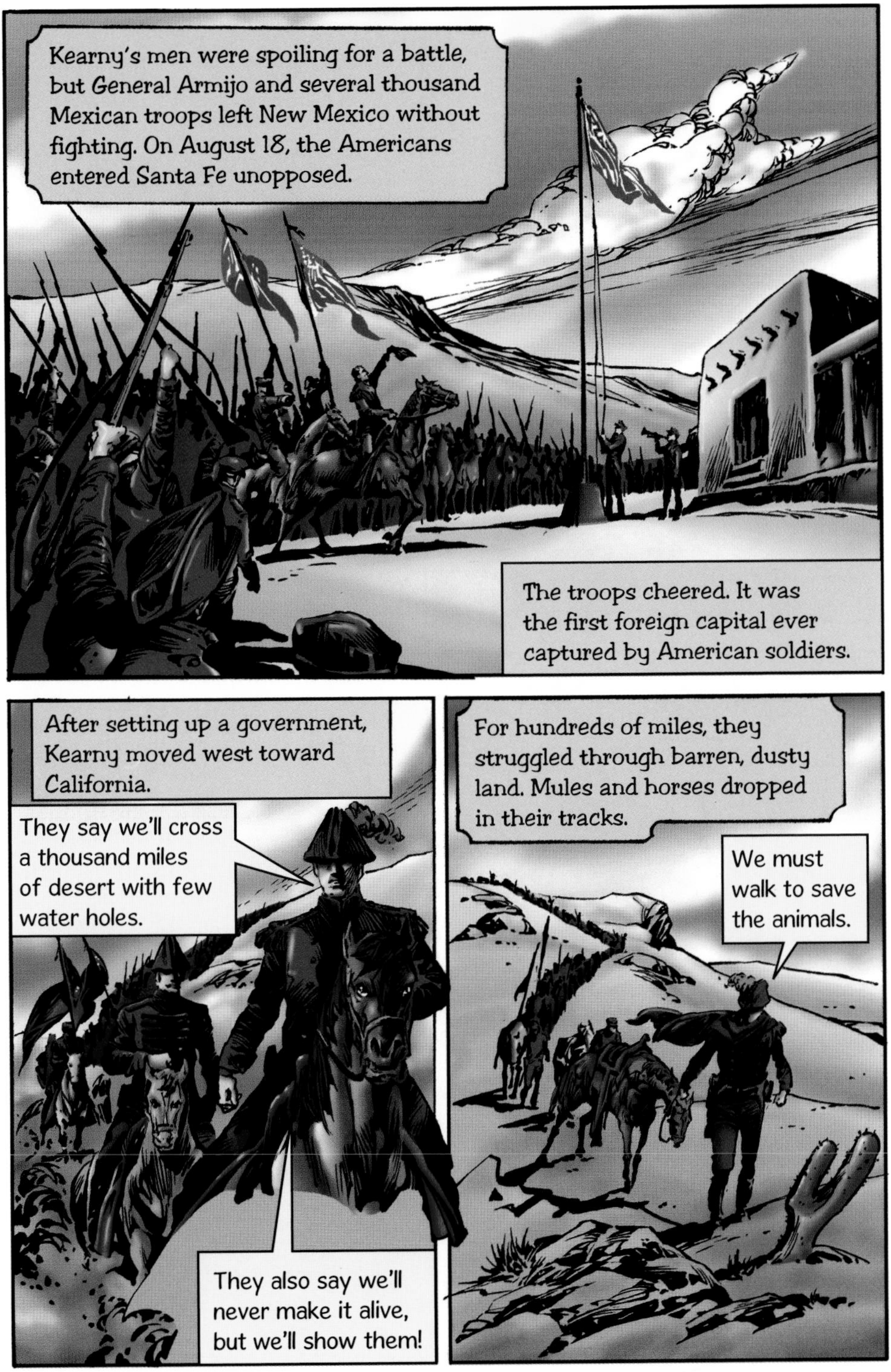
Kearny's men were spoiling for a battle, but General Armijo and several thousand Mexican troops left New Mexico without fighting. On August 18, the Americans entered Santa Fe unopposed.
The troops cheered. It was the first foreign capital ever captured by American soldiers.
After setting up a government, Kearny moved west toward California.
They say we'll cross a thousand miles of desert with few water holes.
They also say we'll never make it alive, but we'll show them!
For hundreds of miles, they struggled through barren, dusty land. Mules and horses dropped in their tracks.
We must walk to save the animals.

Meanwhile in California, a group of American settlers revolted. They seized the village of Sonoma and raised a home-made flag.

We hereby proclaim the Republic of California!

Hurray for the Bear Flag Republic!

But the Mexicans fought back. When Kearny and his exhausted men pushed out of the mountains, they were attacked.

Not only did the attackers' long lances outreach the dragoons' sabers, but they also skillfully used their lassos.

In this, the bloodiest battle fought on California soil, 19 of Kearny's men were killed and 25 wounded. But the Mexicans withdrew without pressing their advantage. United States Navy forces from San Diego arrived to help. Eventually, the Mexicans were defeated and all resistance in California ended.

On February 2, 1848, a peace treaty was signed. Mexico ceded to the United States all land north of the Rio Grande and Gila rivers, for which we paid $15,000,000.

Daniel Webster, the great New England orator, made a rash statement.

California is not worth a single dollar!

CEDED BY GREAT BRITAIN 1818

BOUNDARY TREATY OF 1846

OREGON COUNTRY 1846

LOUISIANA PURCHASE 1803

ACQUIRED DURING THE REVOLUTION AND BY TREATY OF 1783

MEXICAN CESSION 1848

ORIGINAL THIRTEEN STATES

TEXAN ANNEXATION 1845

GADSDEN PURCHASE 1853

SPANISH CESSION 1819

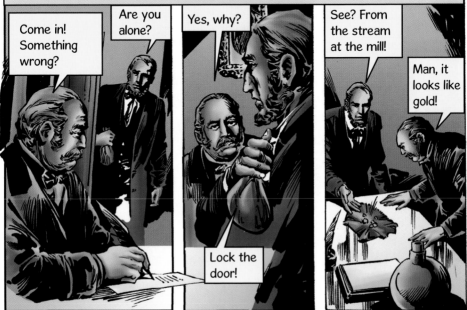

John Sutter, a Swiss adventurer, owned 50,000 acres of California land. He hired John Marshall to build a sawmill there. One rainy day in January 1848, Marshall knocked at Sutter's door.

Come in! Something wrong?

Are you alone?

Yes, why?

Lock the door!

See? From the stream at the mill!

Man, it looks like gold!

Sutter tried to keep the strike a secret but the word spread, and men poured into California from all over the world.

Those who reached the mountains in 1848 found gold in great amounts—in streams, gravel beds, rocks.

A strike! Gold! I'm rich!

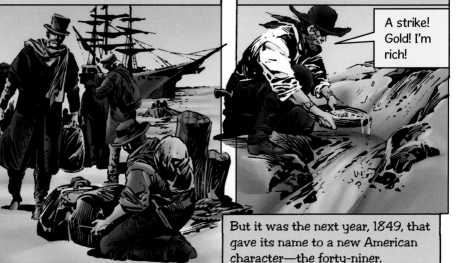

But it was the next year, 1849, that gave its name to a new American character—the forty-niner.

Some people made their money from selling scarce supplies to the miners.

Eggs, one dollar each. Bread, 50 cents. Boots, $100! That's money!

You can't get them anywhere else for less.

Some struck it rich. Many had hard luck. But California was settled quickly, for most who came stayed there.

I didn't do so well mining gold, but I found some good land to farm.

During 1849, the population increased from 20,000 to 100,000. In 1850, California became a state.

Most people still moved west not because of gold, but for the chance to own their own land. In Europe the dream of coming to America was so common, it was known as the American Fever.

In Norway, people read the *America Book* by Ole Rynning.

The best time to leave for America is early in the spring, so that in the new settlement something can be planted the first year.

In Norway, there are too many people! The government takes all we can earn! We must go to America!

Between 1820 and 1860, about 80,000 Norwegians came to America and 90% of them became farmers.

In Sweden, so many people left for America that the government tried to pass laws forbidding it.

In Sweden, a few rich men own all the good land. We must go to America!

Emigrants came from the German states, and from the poorest country of all, Ireland. The Germans were the second and the Irish the third largest national groups in America. They came to the land of opportunity, where a man could hope to own land, work for a living wage, build railroads, build cities, grow and prosper with the country.

But to one group of Americans, this dream was only a threat. Again and again Tecumsah had warned his people.

General Harrison, who had led the American troops, summed up the settlers' viewpoint.

Unless the Indian peoples unite against the white invader, our last hunting grounds will be taken from us. We will all be driven toward the setting sun!

Is one of the fairest portions of the globe to remain the haunt of a few wretched savages, when it seems destined to support a large population, and to be the seat of civilization?

But Tecumsah had died fighting for the British in the War of 1812.

The removal of the northern Native Americans to lands west of the Mississippi was largely accomplished between 1829 and 1843.

The 19,000 Indians of the Cherokee Nation were a different sort. By 1800, living on lands largely in Georgia, they had been at peace for two generations. Many had intermarried with whites. They were planters, hunters, farmers, slave owners—a prosperous people.

In 1821, John Ross, chairman of the Tribal Council, met with Sequoyah, another Cherokee.

Ross had been educated at Dartmouth College. He knew Latin, Greek, English, French, Spanish. But many Cherokees had no written language.

You say you have important news?

I have developed a written Cherokee language. I can read it and write it. I can teach it to others.

No tribes have ever developed a true written language! Will you demonstrate this thing to the council?

Sequoyah's invention became the Cherokee national language. Because of it, great things happened to the Cherokee Nation. In 1828, the council met to honor Sequoyah.

Thanks to you, we now have a national press, a national newspaper, a national magazine, our own school system! We name you an adviser of the Nation— and award you an annual pension!

But Sequoyah had a warning for Ross.

I have moved the Cherokee Nation west to the Arkansas Territory. We cannot hold the lands here much longer! White settlers are pushing in ...

But we own this land by law! By treaties with the United States!

No treaties will hold the white flood back forever. Better to go willingly than to be forced!

In 1830, Congress passed an Indian Removal Act. The Cherokees and other southern tribes were ordered to move to lands in the West. The Cherokees refused to go. In 1838, regular army troops under General Scott rounded them up and escorted them on the long march to Indian Territory, now known as the "Trail of Tears."

Heat, cold, hunger, and disease caused the deaths of one-fourth of the Cherokees before the ten-month ordeal was over.

Most Americans still lived in rural areas, and most farm families worked hard. In Franklin, Massachusetts, in 1802, there lived six-year-old Horace Mann, his father, mother, brothers, and sisters.

Son, your father and Stanley and Stephen have been plowing since early day. Take them this water.

Here, I'll help!

Thanks, Stephen.

In this field we'll plant corn. And over there, hay for the animals.

Stephen was eight years old. His special job was the kitchen garden, which supplied the family vegetables.

Can't you come play with me?

I'm too big now. Next year the garden will be your job and I'll help in the fields.

What Horace wanted most was to go to school and learn to read, so he was glad when summer ended.

The hay is in, the corn is in the loft. There'll be frost tonight.

The last vegetables are gathered and stored. I must busy myself with the weaving.

While his mother wove wool from their sheep into cloth for jackets and trousers, his father made new slate frames.

If I can learn to read, I don't care.

You won't need a slate this year Horace, but I'll be learning to write.

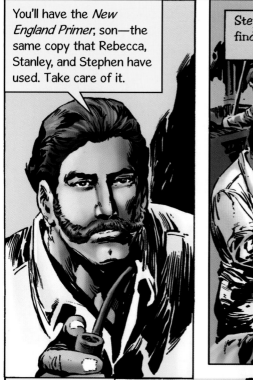

You'll have the *New England Primer*, son—the same copy that Rebecca, Stanley, and Stephen have used. Take care of it.

Stephen saved the best quill he could find from their flock of geese.

Stanley showed me how to make a good pen.

And I am making you a copybook, Stephen.

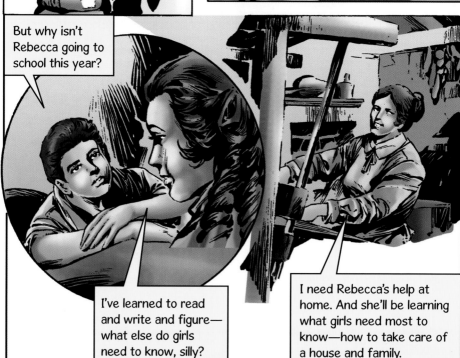

But why isn't Rebecca going to school this year?

I've learned to read and write and figure— what else do girls need to know, silly?

I need Rebecca's help at home. And she'll be learning what girls need most to know—how to take care of a house and family.

The first day of school, Horace was excited and scared.

Beginners, come to the front. I will hear your A, B, Cs.

Repeat after me: ab—eb—ib—ob—ub.

ab—eb—ib—ob—ub.

Horace was disappointed. How would this teach him to read? He didn't learn even one word.

Gradually, Horace did learn. Four years passed quickly. Stanley left school to help his father, but Stephen and Horace did well. Still Horace was not satisfied.

There are so many things I want to know that the schoolmaster doesn't teach us! Sometimes I think he doesn't know too much!

The last day of school was examination day, conducted by the minister. Afterward, Stephen had exciting news.

How did you do today, Stephen?

Very well, sir! Dr. Emmons said I should go to an academy and prepare for college!

I am glad you did well, son. But academics are not for farmer's sons. We can never afford it.

Why, we can hardly buy the books you boys need for the district school.

Later, the boys talked.

In the district school we can never learn what we need to know for college.

I don't want to be a farmer. Why shouldn't poor children have a chance to learn?

Horace liked Sundays because there was time to think. Only the most necessary chores were done. Nobody cooked hot meals.

The carriage is ready.

Careful with the food boys!

At church, Horace and Stephen sat in the boys' corner of the balcony.

But sometimes the hours of the morning service seemed very long.

At noon, the families gathered in the noon rooms across from the church.

Then it was back to the church again for the afternoon services.

Do try some of my cookies!

Ground's still a mite wet for plowing.

Yes, a late spring season.

It was years before Horace Mann was able to complete his education. Starting when he was 20 years old, he did preparatory work, went to college, and went to law school. He became a successful lawyer and was elected to the Massachusetts Senate. In 1837, the Senate passed a bill creating a state board of education.

One day, Mann was offered a new job.

He made a speaking tour of the cities and towns.

Mr. Mann, we need a secretary for the new board of education. You are best fitted for the job. Will you accept?

When I think of my own long struggle, and the poor children who need an education, how can I refuse?

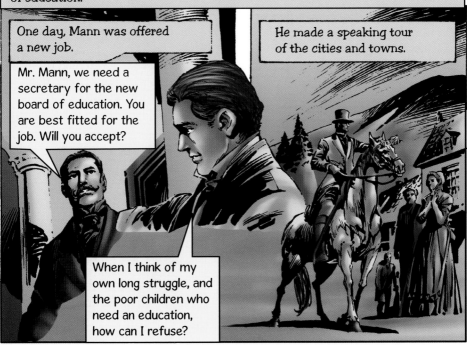

The best way to guard our freedom is to educate all the people!

We must have good free schools—and people must be required to send their children!

For good schools, we need good teachers. We must have teacher training schools.

Many people opposed Mann's ideas. But he and others talked and worked to prove their theories. Gradually, the idea of compulsory free public education for every young American took hold.

In 1852, Mann became president of the new Antioch College, in Ohio.

Oberlin College was the first to admit women in 1837. We want them at Antioch, too!

Many people believe this will not work!

The first class graduated in 1857.

I am proud that the class of 1857 numbers three young ladies among its graduates!

Most people still considered that women did not need so much education. The only profession in which they were really accepted was teaching. It took Elizabeth Blackwell's determination to change that.

Brother Henry, nothing will change my mind. I must be a doctor!

My dear Elizabeth, I will help you any way I can.

Elizabeth was well qualified. She applied to the best medical schools.

Philadelphia, Boston, New York—they all say "impossible"! Women cannot be doctors!

Perhaps one of the smaller schools?

The smaller schools have turned me down, also. There is only one I haven't heard from.

Perhaps this one?

Henry! It ... they ... I can't read it!

"... the application of Elizabeth Blackwell meets with our approval." Geneva Medical College accepts you!

The course had already begun. Elizabeth hurried to Geneva, New York, where she looked for a rooming house.

I run a very correct house! It would ruin me to rent you a room!

No matter what your views on female education, my conduct will be blameless!

In the town, she was a nine days' wonder.

Doctor, doctor in petticoats ... Do you cure corns or do you cure goats?

At the school, too, there was trouble with both faculty and students. But she did not care as long as she could learn.

In the treatment of cholera, we can do very little. Whether we use leaching, cupping, or bloodletting, the disease runs its course.

There is so much about the body we don't know! We must learn how to cure disease—also how to prevent it.

But sometimes there was news of medical advances.

At Massachusetts General Hospital in Boston, Dr. W.T.G. Norton demonstrated the use of a general anaesthesia! Chloroform or ether are inhaled, putting the patient to sleep and making surgery less painful!

In 1849, for the first time in the history of medical education, a woman was given a diploma from a medical college.

It shall be the effort of my life to shed honor upon your diploma!

For two years Elizabeth studied further in Paris. In 1851, she returned to New York, hoping to practice medicine there.

As she fought for the acceptance of women in medicine, others fought in other fields, among them Elizabeth Stanton and Lucretia Mott.

New York has become a great city. Among its 300,000 people, surely some will accept a woman doctor!

All God's children are equal. Women should have the same chances, the same legal rights as men.

And we must have the vote!

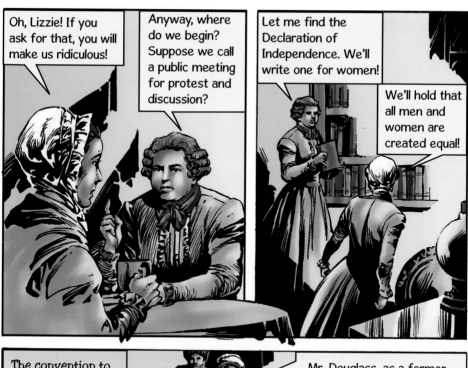

Oh, Lizzie! If you ask for that, you will make us ridiculous!

Anyway, where do we begin? Suppose we call a public meeting for protest and discussion?

Let me find the Declaration of Independence. We'll write one for women!

We'll hold that all men and women are created equal!

The convention to draw up a women's Declaration of Independence was held in Seneca Falls, New York, in 1848. Both women and men attended.

Mr. Douglass, as a former slave, tell me—what do blacks need most to win their rights?

The ballot! The vote!

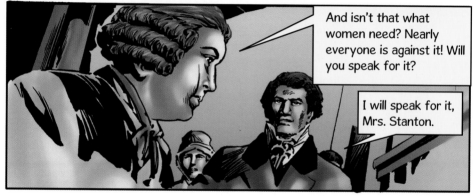

And isn't that what women need? Nearly everyone is against it! Will you speak for it?

I will speak for it, Mrs. Stanton.

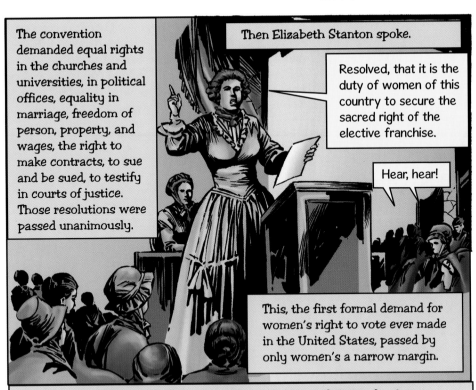

The convention demanded equal rights in the churches and universities, in political offices, equality in marriage, freedom of person, property, and wages, the right to make contracts, to sue and be sued, to testify in courts of justice. Those resolutions were passed unanimously.

Then Elizabeth Stanton spoke.

Resolved, that it is the duty of women of this country to secure the sacred right of the elective franchise.

Hear, hear!

This, the first formal demand for women's right to vote ever made in the United States, passed by only women's a narrow margin.

Conventions followed in other states. Many who were fighting for the abolition of slavery also joined the fight for women's rights.

In Akron, Ohio, in 1851, men tried to takeover a women's-rights convention, causing a near riot.

At last a black woman who had once been a slave moved to the front and spoke.

That man says women need to be helped into carriages and have the best place everywhere.

Booooooo! Go home, ladies! Take care of your husbands and babies!

Order! Order! Please!

44

Nobody helps me into carriages, or over mud puddles, or gives me any best place. And ain't I a woman?

Look at my arm! I have plowed and planted and gathered into barns as well as any man—and borne the lash as well! And ain't I a woman?

I have borne 13 children and seen most of them sold off to slavery, and when I cried out my mother's grief none but Jesus heard me. And ain't I a woman?

First there was silence, then great applause. This was Isabella Truth, who became known to abolitionist and women's rights audiences as Sojourner Truth.

One of the hardest jobs on a farm had always been cutting grain with a scythe.

In 1831, Cyrus McCormick invented and demonstrated a horse-drawn reaper.

Bedogged, if I ever saw anything to beat that!

I guess it can do the work of 10 men.

Soon, McCormick was selling several thousand reapers a year.

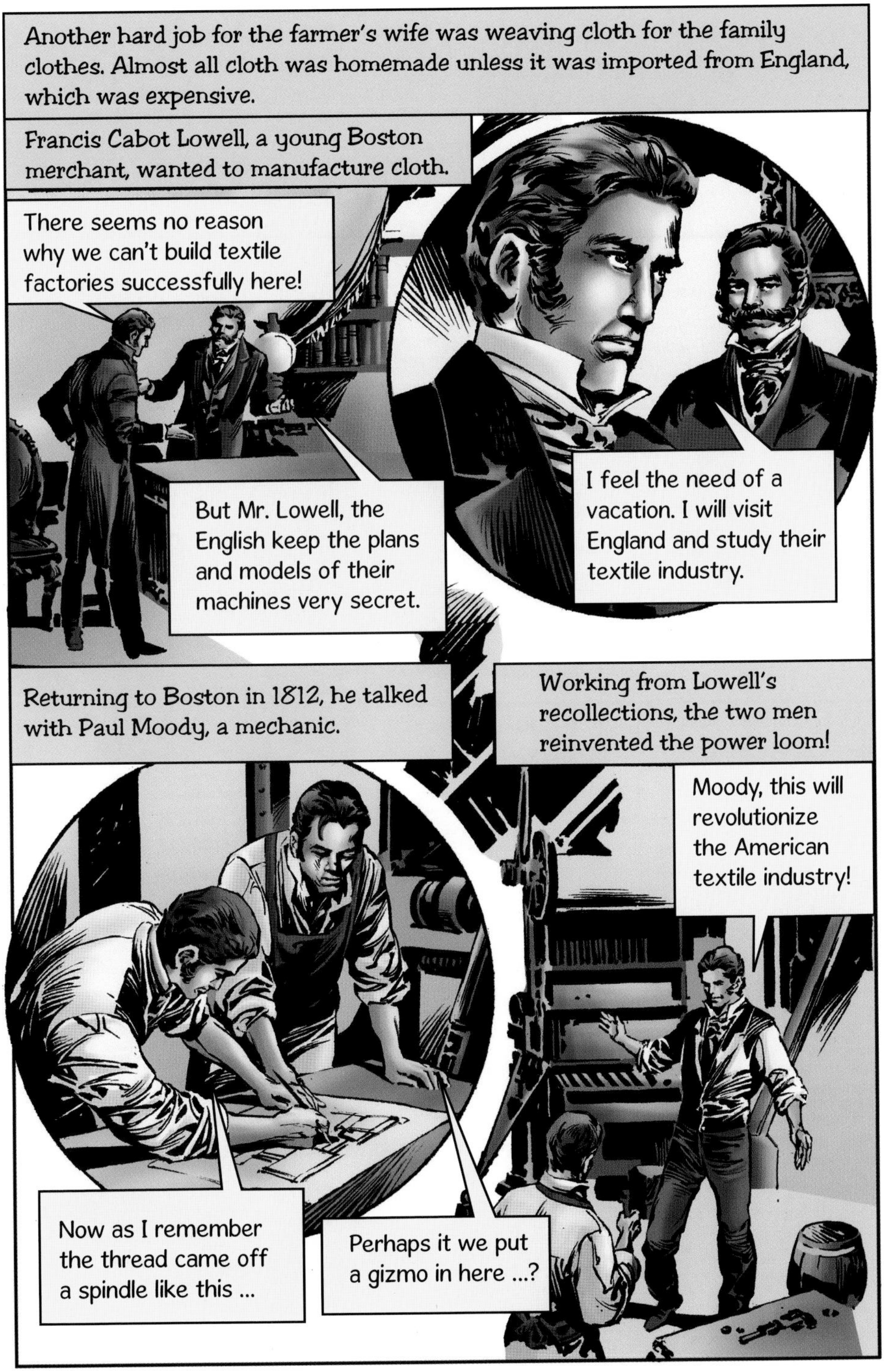
Another hard job for the farmer's wife was weaving cloth for the family clothes. Almost all cloth was homemade unless it was imported from England, which was expensive.
Francis Cabot Lowell, a young Boston merchant, wanted to manufacture cloth.
There seems no reason why we can't build textile factories successfully here!
But Mr. Lowell, the English keep the plans and models of their machines very secret.
I feel the need of a vacation. I will visit England and study their textile industry.
Returning to Boston in 1812, he talked with Paul Moody, a mechanic.
Now as I remember the thread came off a spindle like this ...
Perhaps it we put a gizmo in here ...?
Working from Lowell's recollections, the two men reinvented the power loom!
Moody, this will revolutionize the American textile industry!

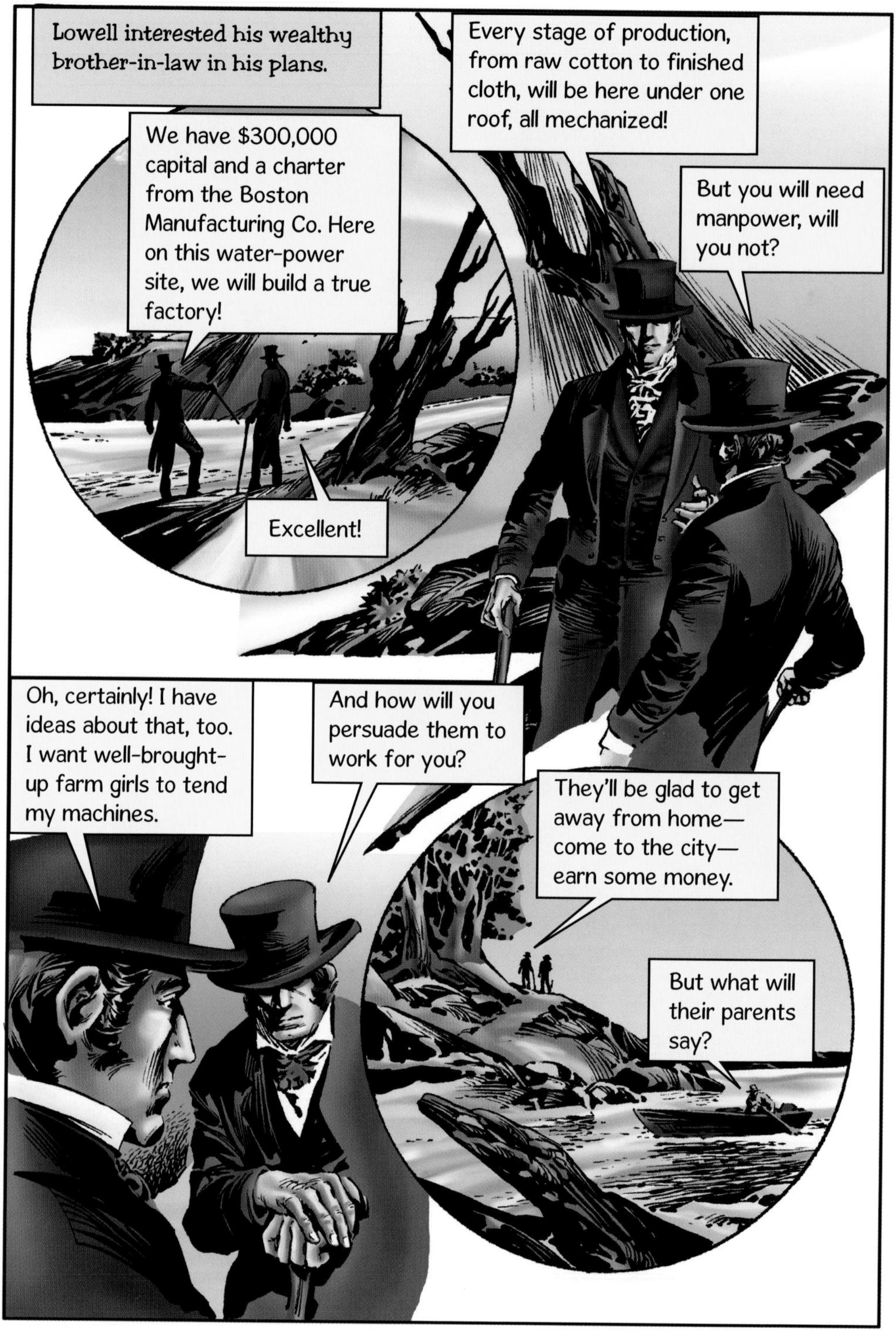
Lowell interested his wealthy brother-in-law in his plans.
We have $300,000 capital and a charter from the Boston Manufacturing Co. Here on this water-power site, we will build a true factory!
Excellent!
Every stage of production, from raw cotton to finished cloth, will be here under one roof, all mechanized!
But you will need manpower, will you not?
Oh, certainly! I have ideas about that, too. I want well-brought-up farm girls to tend my machines.
And how will you persuade them to work for you?
They'll be glad to get away from home— come to the city— earn some money.
But what will their parents say?

The girls came, too. By 1831 the company had seven more factories on the Merrimac River. Some 2,500 Lowell girls were in the mills, in a new town named Lowell.

New Hampshire, up in the White Mountains. And I had to work a lot harder there on the farm!

So did I at home!

After the first factory was going well, Lowell went to Washington. He talked to Southerners like John C. Calhoun.

Senator, I want to recall to your mind another New Englander, Eli Whitney.

In 1793, Eli Whitney went South to take a job as a tutor. On the way, he stopped off in Georgia to visit friends at Mulberry Grove Plantation. Neighbors dropped in and, as usual, the talk turned to the hard times.

The trouble is, we have no money crop!

What about cotton!

The only kind that will grow here is practically useless. It takes ten hours of hard work to separate a pound of lint from three pounds of seeds. Unless we find a machine for the work, it's little better than a weed.

Gentlemen, speak to my young friend, Mr. Whitney. He can make anything.

I like to make things. Could I watch somebody clean cotton by hand?

Yes, indeed! Come along.

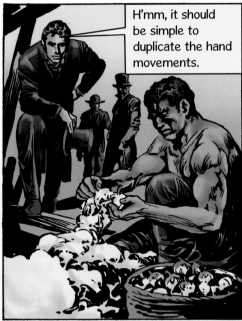

H'mm, it should be simple to duplicate the hand movements.

For several days Whitney thought about it.

If I had a sieve of fine wires to hold the cotton...

Aww-w-w-w-K!

... and a set of sharp little hooks to catch the fibers!

A sieve, a revolving drum with small, sharp hooks, and a brush to clean the hooks—this was Whitney's cotton engine, or "gin."

When I turn the crank, out comes the cotton!

Eureka! It works!

It will be a great success! We must get some gentlemen in for a demonstration.

The guests were impressed.

In one hour he has turned out more cotton than several workers can now do in a day!

I will order all my fields planted to cotton. At once!

My slaves were costing me more than they were worth. I was about to get rid of them. But this changes everything!

Cotton growing required large numbers of workmen.

Tending the plants meant long hours of stooping under the hot sun.

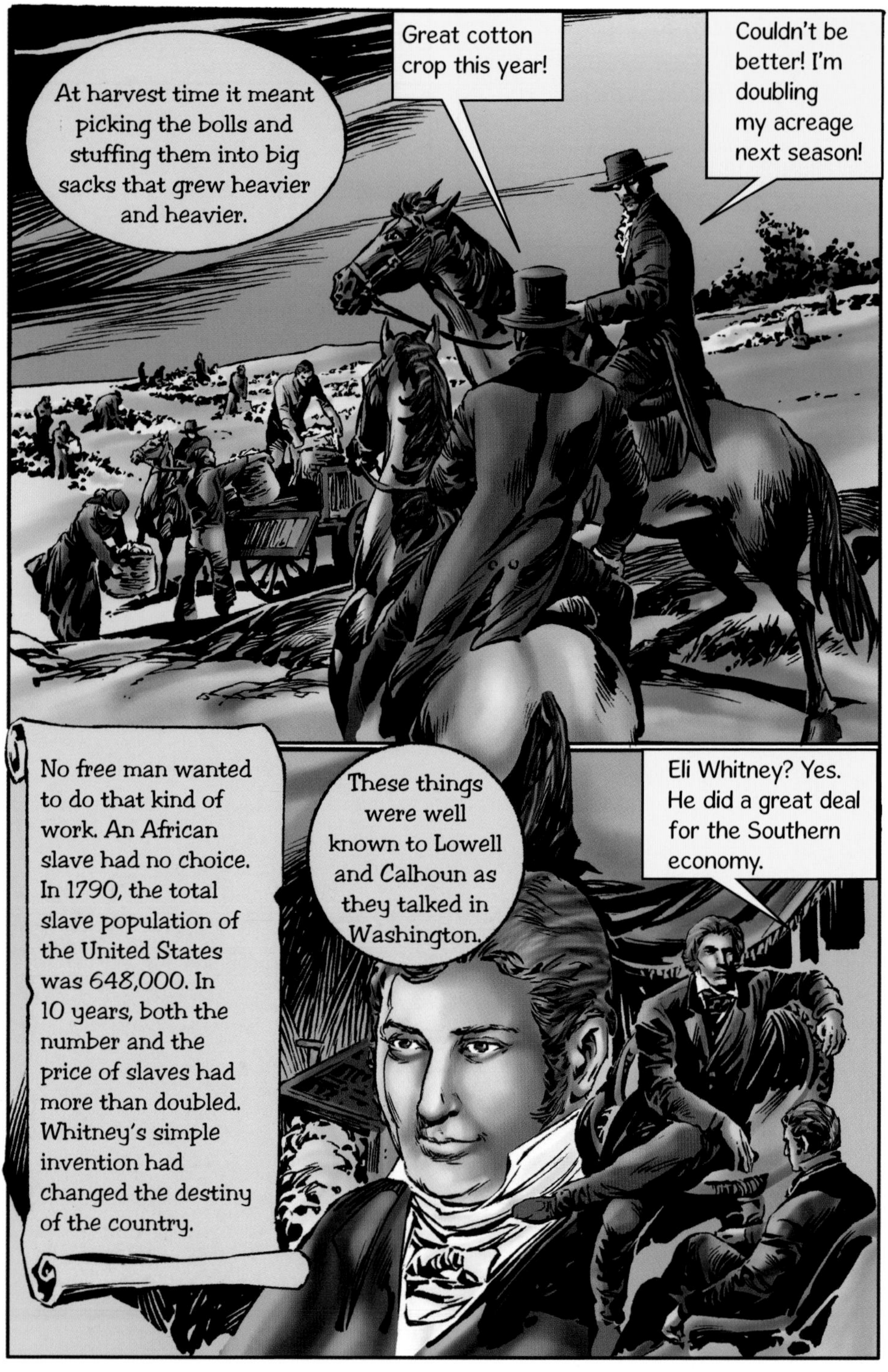
At harvest time it meant picking the bolls and stuffing them into big sacks that grew heavier and heavier.
Great cotton crop this year!
Couldn't be better! I'm doubling my acreage next season!
No free man wanted to do that kind of work. An African slave had no choice. In 1790, the total slave population of the United States was 648,000. In 10 years, both the number and the price of slaves had more than doubled. Whitney's simple invention had changed the destiny of the country.
These things were well known to Lowell and Calhoun as they talked in Washington.
Eli Whitney? Yes. He did a great deal for the Southern economy.

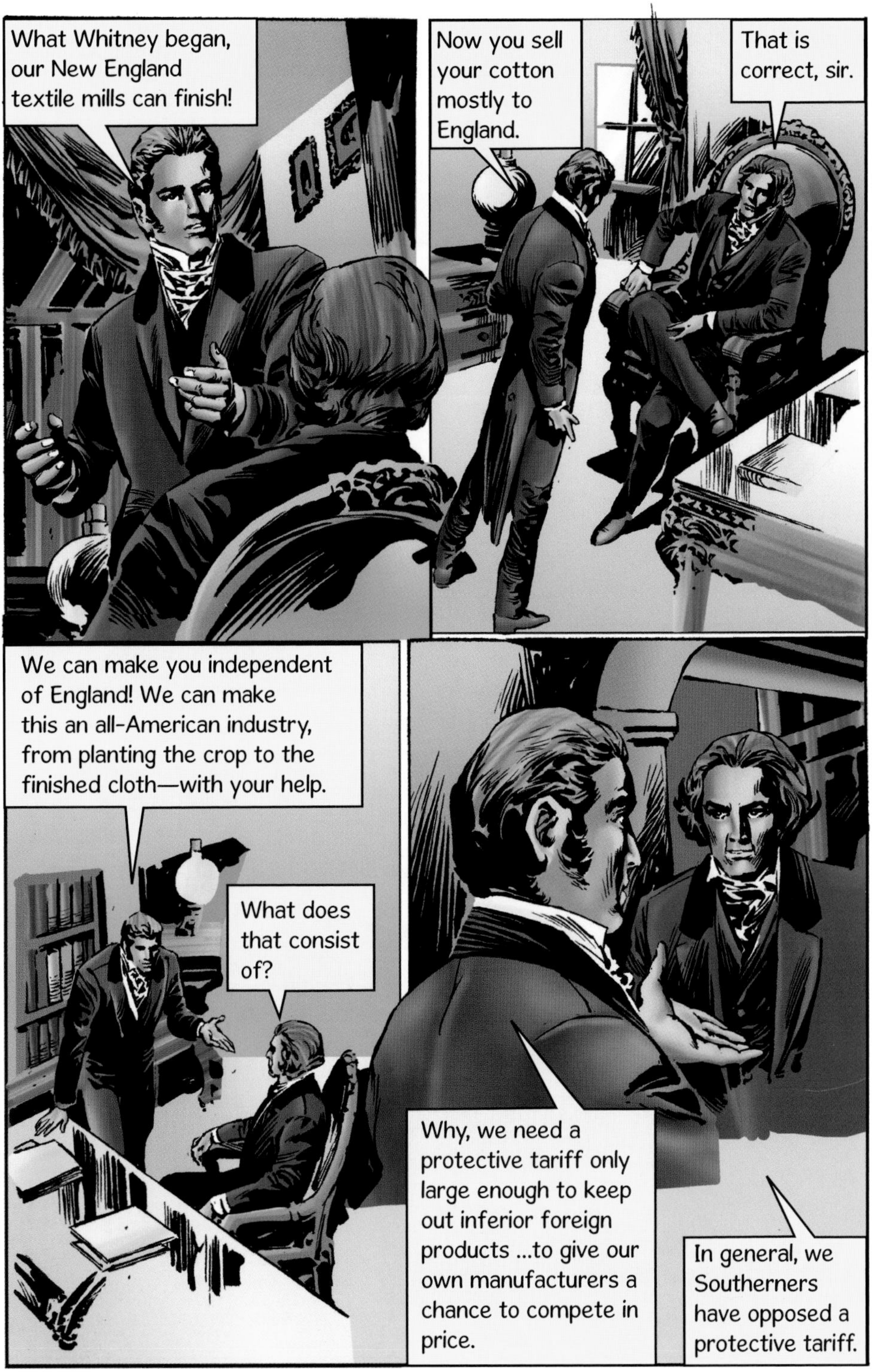
What Whitney began, our New England textile mills can finish!
Now you sell your cotton mostly to England.
That is correct, sir.
We can make you independent of England! We can make this an all-American industry, from planting the crop to the finished cloth—with your help.
What does that consist of?
Why, we need a protective tariff only large enough to keep out inferior foreign products ...to give our own manufacturers a chance to compete in price.
In general, we Southerners have opposed a protective tariff.

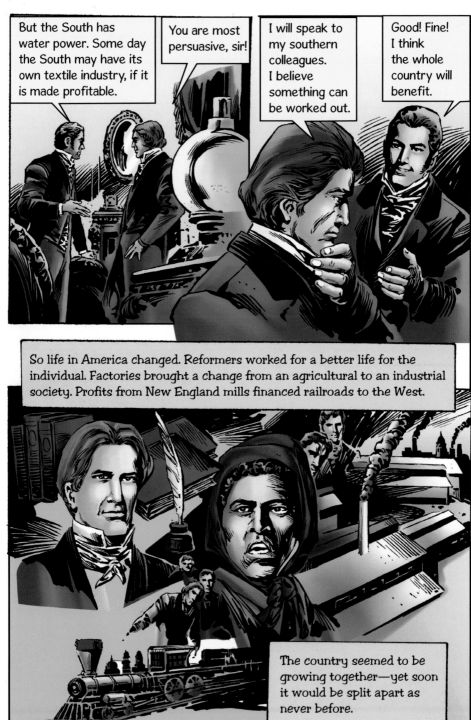

But the South has water power. Some day the South may have its own textile industry, if it is made profitable.

You are most persuasive, sir!

I will speak to my southern colleagues. I believe something can be worked out.

Good! Fine! I think the whole country will benefit.

So life in America changed. Reformers worked for a better life for the individual. Factories brought a change from an agricultural to an industrial society. Profits from New England mills financed railroads to the West.

The country seemed to be growing together—yet soon it would be split apart as never before.